by John Updike

TELEPHONE POLES

and Other Poems

John Updike

TELEPHONE POLES

POLES

and Other Poems

Alfred A. Knopf · New York
1965

ion, forty-seven were
ᴇʀ. Acknowledgment
ᴇs, which first printed

ie at Versailles in
Saints Nouveaux;
Vermont.

Tʜᴇ Cᴏᴍᴍᴏɴᴡᴇᴀʟ: *Caligula's Dream; Erotic Epi-*
grams; Flirt; Maples in a Spruce Forest.

Tʜᴇ Nᴇᴡ Rᴇᴘᴜʙʟɪᴄ: *Deities and Beasts; Tome-*
Thoughts, from the Times.

Sʏʀᴀᴄᴜsᴇ 10: *How to Be Uncle Sam; Trees Eat*
Sunshine.

Wʜᴀᴛ's Nᴇᴡ: *Pop Smash, Out of Echo Chamber.*

Tʜᴇ Cʜʀɪsᴛɪᴀɴ Cᴇɴᴛᴜʀʏ: *Seven Stanzas at Easter.*

Aᴍᴇʀɪᴄᴀɴ Sᴄʜᴏʟᴀʀ: *Calendar.*

L. C. catalog card number: 63–11047

THIS IS A BORZOI BOOK
PUBLISHED BY ALFRED A. KNOPF, INC.

PUBLISHED SEPTEMBER 16, 1963
SECOND PRINTING, DECEMBER 1963
THIRD PRINTING, MARCH 1964
FOURTH PRINTING, AUGUST 1965

TO E. B. AND K. S. WHITE

in gratitude for good example and kind counsel

CONTENTS

I

CONTENTS

II

CONTENTS

I

BENDIX

This porthole overlooks a sea
Forever falling from the sky,
The water inextricably
Involved with buttons, suds, and dye.

Like bits of shrapnel, shards of foam
Fly heavenward; a bedsheet heaves,
A stocking wrestles with a comb,
And cotton angels wave their sleeves.

The boiling purgatorial tide
Revolves our dreary shorts and slips,
While Mother coolly bakes beside
Her little jugged apocalypse.

REEL

Whirl, whorl or wharve! The world
Whirls within solar rings
Which once were hotly hurled
Away by whirling things!

Wind whirls; hair curls; the worm
Can turn, and wheels can wheel,
And even stars affirm:
Whatever whirls is real.

We whirl, or seem to whirl,
Or seem to seem to; whorls
Within more whorls unfurl
In manners, habits, morals.

And when we go and carve
An onion or a tree,
We find, within, a wharve
And, in the wharve, a whee!

COSMIC GALL

Every second, hundreds of billions of these neu-
trinos pass through each square inch of our bodies,
coming from above during the day and from be-
low at night, when the sun is shining on the other
side of the earth!
> —*From "An Explanatory Statement on
> Elementary Particle Physics," by
> M. A. Ruderman and A. H. Rosen-
> feld, in American Scientist.*

Neutrinos, they are very small.
   They have no charge and have no mass
And do not interact at all.
The earth is just a silly ball
   To them, through which they simply pass,
Like dustmaids down a drafty hall
   Or photons through a sheet of glass.
   They snub the most exquisite gas,
Ignore the most substantial wall,
   Cold-shoulder steel and sounding brass,
Insult the stallion in his stall,
   And, scorning barriers of class,
Infiltrate you and me! Like tall
And painless guillotines, they fall
   Down through our heads into the grass.
At night, they enter at Nepal
   And pierce the lover and his lass
From underneath the bed—you call
   It wonderful; I call it crass.

IN PRAISE OF $(C_{10}H_9O_5)_x$

I have now worn the same terylene tie every day
for eighteen months.
—*From "Chemistry," a Penguin book by
Kenneth Hutton*

My tie is made of terylene;
  Eternally I wear it,
For time can never wither, stale,
  Shred, shrink, fray, fade, or tear it.
The storms of January fail
  To loosen it with bluster;
The rains of April fail to stain
  Its polyester lustre;
July's hot sun beats down in vain;
  October's frosts fall futilely;
December's snow can blow and blow—
  My tie remains acutely
Immutable! When I'm below,
  Dissolving in that halcyon
Retort, my carbohydrates shed
  From off my frame of calcium—
When I am, in lay language, dead,
  Across my crumbling sternum
Shall lie a spanking fresh cravat
  Unsullied *ad æternum,*
A grave and solemn prospect that
  Makes light of our allotted
Three score and ten, for terylene
  Shall never be unknotted.

THE DESCENT OF MR. ALDEZ

Mr. Aldez, a cloud physicist, came down last year
to study airborne ice crystals.
    —Dispatch from Antarctica in the Times

That cloud—ambiguous, not
a horse, or a whale, but what?—
comes down through the crystalline mist.
It is a physicist!

Like fog, on cat's feet, tiptoeing
to where the bits of ice are blowing,
it drifts, and eddies, and spies
its prey through vaporous eyes

and pounces! With billowing paws
the vague thing smokily claws
the fluttering air, notes its traits,
smiles knowingly, and dissipates.

CALIGULA'S DREAM

Insomnia was his worst torment. Three hours a night of fitful sleep was all that he ever got, and even then terrifying visions would haunt him— once, for instance, he dreamed that he had a con- versation with the Mediterranean Sea.

—*Suetonius*

Of gold the bread on which he banqueted,
Where pimps in silk and pearls dissolved in wine
Were standard fare. The monster's marble head
Had many antic veins, being divine.
At war, he massed his men upon the beach
And bawled the coward's order, "Gather shells!"
And stooped, in need of prisoners, to teach
The German tongue to prostituted Gauls.
Bald young, broad-browed and, for his era, tall,
In peace he proved incestuous and queer,
And spent long hours in the Capitol
Exchanging compliments with Jupiter;
He stalled his horse in ivory, and displayed
His wife undressed to friends, and liked to view
Eviscerations and the dance, and made
Poor whores supply imperial revenue.

Perhaps—to plead—the boy had heard how when
They took his noble father from the pyre
And found a section unconsumed, the men
Suspicioned: "Poisoned hearts resist the fire."

It was as water that his vision came,
At any rate—more murderous than he,
More wanton, uglier, of wider fame,
Unsleeping also, multi-sexed, the Sea.

It told him, "Little Boots, you cannot sin
Enough; you speak a language, though you rave.
The actual things at home beneath my skin
Out-horrify the vilest hopes you have.
Ten-tentacled invertebrates embrace
And swap through thirsty ana livid seed
While craggy worms without a brain or face
Upon their own soft children blindly feed.
As huge as Persian palaces, blue whales
Grin fathoms down, and through their teeth are strained
A million lives a minute; each entails,
In death, a microscopic bit of pain.
Atrocity is truly emperor;
All things that thrive are slaves of cruel Creation."

Caligula, his mouth a mass of fur,
Awoke, and toppled toward assassination.

WHITE DWARF

Discovery of the smallest known star in the universe was announced today . . . The star is about one half the diameter of the moon.
—*The Times*

Welcome, welcome, little star!
I'm delighted that you are
Up in Heaven's vast extent,
No bigger than a continent.

Relatively minuscule,
Spinning like a penny spool,
Glinting like a polished spoon,
A kind of kindled demi-moon,

You offer cheer to tiny Man
'Mid galaxies Gargantuan—
A little pill in endless night,
An antidote to cosmic fright.

TOOTHACHE MAN

The earth has been unkind to him.
  He lies in middle strata.
The time capsules about him brim
  With advertising matter.

His addled fossils tell a tale
  That lacks barbaric splendor;
His vertebrae are small and pale,
  His femora are slender.

It is his teeth—strange, cratered things—
  That name him. Some are hollow,
Like bowls, and hold gold offerings.
  The god may be Apollo.

Silver and gold. We think he thought
  His god, who was immortal,
Dwelt in his skull; hence, the devout
  Adorned the temple's portal.

Heraldic fists and spears and bells
  In all metallic colors
Invade the bone; their volume swells
  On backward through the molars.

This culture's meagre sediments
  Have come to light just lately.
We handle them with reverence.
  He must have suffered greatly.

DEITIES AND BEASTS

Tall Atlas, Jupiter, Hercules, Thor,
Just like the antic pagan gods of yore,
Make up a too-erratic pantheon
For mortal men to be dependent on.

I much prefer, myself, the humble RAT,
The tiny Terrier, the short Hawk that
Makes secret flight, and the Sparrow, whose fall
Is never mentioned in the press at all.

SONIC BOOM

I'm sitting in the living room,
When, up above, the Thump of Doom
Resounds. Relax. It's sonic boom.

The ceiling shudders at the clap,
The mirrors tilt, the rafters snap,
And Baby wakens from his nap.

"Hush, babe. Some pilot we equip,
Giving the speed of sound the slip,
Has cracked the air like a penny whip."

Our world is far from frightening; I
No longer strain to read the sky
Where moving fingers (jet planes) fly.
Our world seems much too tame to die.

And if it does, with one more *pop,*
I shan't look up to see it drop.

PARTY KNEE

To drink in moderation, and to smoke
  A minimal amount, and joke
  Reservedly does not insure
Awaking from a party whole and pure.

Be we as temperate as the turtledove,
  A soiree is an orgy of
  This strange excess, unknown in France,
And Rome, and Nineveh: the upright stance.

When more than four forgather in our land,
  We stand, and stand, and stand, and stand;
  Thighs ache, and drowsy numbness locks
The bones between our pockets and our socks.

Forgive us, Prince of Easement, when from bed
  With addled knees and lucid head
  We leap at dawn, and sob, and beg
A buffered aspirin for a splitting leg.

THOUGHTS
WHILE DRIVING HOME

Was I clever enough? Was I charming?
Did I make at least one good pun?
Was I disconcerting? Disarming?
Was I wise? Was I wan? Was I fun?

Did I answer that girl with white shoulders
Correctly, or should I have said
(Engagingly), "Kierkegaard smolders,
But Eliot's ashes are dead"?

And did I, while being a smarty,
Yet some wry reserve slyly keep,
So they murmured, when I'd left the party,
"He's deep. He's deep. He's deep"?

IDYLL

Within a quad of aging brick,
Behind the warty warden oak,
The Radcliffe sophomores exchange,
In fencing costume, stroke for stroke;
Their bare knees bent, the darlings duel
Like daughters of Dumas and Scott.
Their sneakered feet torment the lawn,
Their skirted derrières stick out.

Beneath the branches, needles glint
Unevenly in dappled sun
As shadowplay and swordplay are
In no time knitted into one;
The metal twitters, girl hacks girl,
Their educated faces caged.
The fake felt hearts and pointless foils
Contain an oddly actual rage.

A SONG OF PATERNAL CARE

A Lithuanian lithographer
    Who lived on lithia water
Was blessed, by lithogenesis,
    With a lithe and lithic daughter.

Said he beneath a lithy tree
    When she'd reached litholysis,
"It's time you thought of lithomarge,
    And even . . . lithophthisis."

She blushed, the lovely lithoglyph,
    And said, "I love a lithsman.*
I feel so litholyte when I'm,"
    She smiled, eliding, "wi' th's man."

"Go fetch the lithofellic fellow!"
    Her father boomed, with laughter.
She did. They lived in Lithgow, Aus.,
    Litherly** ever after.

* An unfortunately obsolete word meaning a sailor in the navy under the Danish kings of England.
** Another, meaning mischievous, wicked, or lazy.

MARRIAGE COUNSEL

WHY MARRY OGRE
JUST TO GET HUBBY?
—*Headline in the Boston Herald*

Why marry ogre
  Just to get hubby?
Has he a brogue, or
  Are his legs stubby?

Smokes he a stogie?
  Is he not sober?
Is he too logy
  And dull as a crowbar?

Tom, Dick, and Harry:
  Garrulous, greedy,
And grouchy. They vary
  From savage to seedy,

And, once wed, will parry
  To be set asunder.
O harpy, why marry
  Ogre? I wonder.

RECITAL

ROGER BOBO GIVES
RECITAL ON TUBA
—Headline in the Times

Eskimos in Manitoba,
  Barracuda off Aruba,
Cock an ear when Roger Bobo
  Starts to solo on the tuba.

Men of every station—Pooh-Bah,
  Nabob, bozo, toff, and hobo—
Cry in unison, "Indubi-
  Tably, there is simply nobo-

Dy who oompahs on the tubo,
Solo, quite like Roger Bubo!"

19

TROPICAL BEETLES

Composed of horny, jagged blacks
   Yet quite unformidable,
They flip themselves upon their backs
   And die beneath the table.

The Temperate wasp, with pointed moan,
   Flies straightway to the apple;
But bugs inside the Tropic Zone
   With idle fancies grapple.

They hurl themselves past window sills
   And labor through a hundred
Ecstatic, crackling, whirring spills—
   For what, I've often wondered.

They seek the light—it stirs their stark,
   Ill-lit imaginations—
And win, when stepped on in the dark,
   Disgusted exclamations.

B. W. I.

Under a priceless sun,
   Shanties and guava.
Beside an emerald sea,
   Lumps of lava.

On the white dirt road,
   A blind man tapping.
On dark Edwardian sofas,
   White men napping.

In half-caste twilight, heartfelt
   Songs to Jesus.
Across the arid land,
   Ocean breezes.
The sibilance of sadness
   Never ceases.

The empty cistern.
   The broken Victrola.
The rusted praise of
   Coca-Cola.

Old yellow tablecloths,
   And tea, and hairy
Goats, and airmail
   Stationery.

Copies of *Punch* and *Ebony*.
   Few flowers.
Just the many-petalled sun above
   The endless hours.

EXPOSURE

Please do not tell me there is no voodoo,
For, if so, how then do you
Explain that a photograph of a head
Always tells if the person is living or dead?

Always. I have never known it to fail.
There is something misted in the eyes, something pale,
If not in the lips, then in the hair—
It is hard to put your finger on, but there.

A kind of third dimension settles in:
A blur, a kiss of otherness, a milky film.
If, while you hold a snapshot of Aunt Flo,
Her real heart stops, you will know.

COMP. RELIGION

It all begins with fear of *mana*.
  Next there comes the love of tribe.
Native dances, totems, ani-
  Mism and magicians thrive.

Culture grows more complicated.
  Spirits, chiefs in funny hats,
And suchlike spooks are sublimated
  Into gods and ziggurats.

Polyarmed and polyheaded,
  Gods proliferate until
Puristic-minded sages edit
  Their welter into one sweet Will.

This worshipped One grows so enlightened,
  Vast, and high He, in a blur,
Explodes; and men are left as frightened
  Of *mana* as they ever were.

BESTIARY

If the transmigration of a soul takes place into a
rational being, it simply becomes the soul of that
body. But if the soul migrates into a brute beast,
it follows the body outside as a guardian spirit
follows a man.

—*Sallustius*

Each bird is chased by another bird,
   Each worm by a shadow worm,
Much as each thing has a word
   Guarding its spirit and form.

These are the rational souls;
   Unable to enter, they float
Behind the brutes, the fishes and fowls,
   As a dory is dragged by a boat.

This accounts for the animal world—
   Its qualms and skittering fears—
For each squirrel feels a rational squirrel
   Pressing on its ears.

THE HIGH-HEARTS

Assumption of erect posture in man lifts the heart
higher above the ground than in any other animal
now living except the giraffe and the elephant.
  —*From an article titled "Anatomy" in the
  Encyclopaedia Britannica*

Proud elephant, by accident of bulk,
Upreared the mammoth cardiacal hulk
That plunged his storm of blood through canvas veins.
Enthroned beneath his tusks, unseen, it reigns
In dark state, stoutly ribbed, suffused with doubt,
Where lions have to leap to seek it out.

Herbivorous giraffe, in dappled love
With green and sunstruck edibles above,
Yearned with his bones; in an aeon or so,
His glad heart left his ankles far below,
And there, where forelegs turn to throat, it trem-
Bles like a blossom halfway up a stem.

Poor man, an ape, anxious to use his paws,
Became erect and held the pose because
His brain, developing beyond his ken,
Kept whispering, "The universe wants men."
So still he strains to keep his heart aloft,
Too high and low at once, too hard and soft.

THE MENAGERIE
AT VERSAILLES IN 1775

Taken verbatim from a notebook kept by
Dr. Samuel Johnson

Cygnets dark; their black feet;
on the ground; tame.
Halcyons, or gulls.
Stag and hind, small.
Aviary, very large: the net, wire.
Black stag of China, small.

Rhinoceros, the horn broken
and pared away, which, I suppose,
will grow; the basis, I think,
four inches 'cross; the skin
folds like loose cloth doubled over his body
and 'cross his hips: a vast animal,
though young; as big, perhaps,
as four oxen.

        The young elephant,
with his tusks just appearing.
The brown bear put out his paws.
All very tame. The lion.
The tigers I did not well view.
The camel, or dromedary with two bunches

called the Huguin, taller than any horse.
Two camels with one bunch.

Among the birds was a pelican,
who being let out, went
to a fountain, and swam
about to catch fish. His feet
well webbed: he dipped his head,
and turned his long bill sidewise.

This passage may be found, in prose and punctuated a bit
differently, on pp. 555–6 of the Modern Library Giant edition
of Boswell's *Life*.

UPON LEARNING THAT
A BIRD EXISTS
CALLED THE TURNSTONE

A turnstone turned rover
And went through ten turnstiles,
Admiring the clover
And turnsole and fern styles.

The Turneresque landscape
She scanned for a lover;
She'd heard one good turnstone
Deserves another.

She took to the turnpike
And travelled to Dover,
Where turnips enjoy
A rapid turnover.

In vain did she hover
And earnestly burn
With yearning; above her
The terns cried, "Return!"

UPON LEARNING THAT
A TOWN EXISTS IN VIRGINIA
CALLED UPPERVILLE

In Upperville, the upper crust
Say "Bottoms up!" from dawn to dusk
And "Ups-a-daisy, dear!" at will—
I want to live in Upperville.

One-upmanship is there the rule,
And children learn about, at school,
"The Rise of Silas Lapham" and
Why gravitation has been banned.

High hamlet, ho!—my mind's eye sees
Thy ruddy uplands, lofty trees,
Upsurging streams, and towering dogs;
There are no valleys, dumps, or bogs.

Depression never dares intrude
Upon thy sweet upswinging mood;
Downcast, long-fallen, let me go
To where the cattle never low.

I've always known there was a town
Just right for me; I'll settle down
And be uplifted all day long—
Fair Upperville, accept my song.

ZULUS LIVE IN LAND
WITHOUT A SQUARE

A Zulu lives in a round world. If he does not leave
his reserve, he can live his whole life through and
never see a straight line.
—*Headline and text from the Times*

In Zululand the huts are round,
The windows oval, and the rooves
Thatched parabolically. The ground
Is tilled in curvilinear grooves.

When Zulus cannot smile, they frown,
To keep an arc before the eye.
Describing distances to town,
They say, "As flies the butterfly."

Anfractuosity is king.
Melodic line itself is banned,
Though all are hep enough to sing—
There are no squares in Zululand.

POP SMASH, OUT OF
ECHO CHAMBER

O truly, Lily was a lulu,
   Doll, and dilly of a belle;
No one's smile was more enamelled,
No one's style was more untrammelled,
   Yet her records failed to sell
      Well.

Her agent, Daley, duly worried,
   Fretted, fidgeted, complained,
Daily grew so somber clever
Wits at parties said whenever
   Lily waxed, poor Daley waned.
      Strained

Beyond endurance, feeling either
   He or Lily must be drowned,
Daley, dulled to Lily's lustre,
Deeply down a well did thrust her.
   Lily yelled; he dug the sound,
      Found

A phone, contacted Victor,
   Cut four sides; they sold, and how!
Daley disclaims credit; still, he
Likes the lucre. As for Lily,
   She is dry and famous now.
      Wow.

THE MODERATE

Frost's space is deeper than Poliakoff's and not as deep as that of Soulages.

—*Patrick Heron in Arts*

"Soulages's space is deep and wide—
Beware!" they said. "Beware," they cried,
"The yawning gap, the black abyss
That closes with a dreadful hiss!

"That shallow space by Poliakoff,"
They added, "is a wretched trough.
It wrinkles, splinters, shreds, and fades;
It wouldn't hold the Jack of Spades."

"But where?" I asked, bewildered, lost.
"Go seek," they said, "the space of Frost;
It's not too bonny, not too braw—
The nicest space you ever saw."

I harked, and heard, and here I live,
Delighted to be relative.   .

KENNETHS

Rexroth and Patchen and Fearing—their mothers
Perhaps could distinguish their sons from the others,
But I am unable. My inner eye pictures
A three-bodied sun-lover issuing strictures,
Berating "Tom" Eliot, translating tanka,
Imbibing espresso and sneering at Sanka—
Six arms, thirty fingers, all writing abundantly
What pops into heads each named Kenneth,
      redundantly.

TOME-THOUGHTS,
FROM THE TIMES

The special merit of the two first novels up for discussion today is that they are neither overly ambitious nor overly long. Both are deftly written, amusing and intensely feminine. Both are the work of brightly talented young women.
—*Orville Prescott, in The New York Times*

Oh, to be Orville Prescott
Now that summer's here,
And the books on tinted paper
Blow lightly down the air,
And the merciful brevity of every page
Becalms the winter's voluminous rage,
And unambition like lilac lies
On Prescott's eyes.

When heroines with small frustrations,
Dressed in transparent motivations,
Glimmer and gambol, trip and trot;
Then may the sensitive critic spy,
Beneath the weave of a gossamer plot,
The subtle pink of an author's thigh.
Oh bliss! oh brightly talented! oh neither
Overly this nor that—a breather!
Along the sands of the summer lists
The feminine first novelists
Go dancing, deft, and blessed twice over
By Prescott, deep in short-stemmed clover.

I MISSED HIS BOOK,
BUT I READ HIS NAME

"The Silver Pilgrimage," by M. Anantanarayanan.
. . . 160 pages. Criterion. $3.95.

—*The Times*

Though authors are a dreadful clan
To be avoided if you can,
I'd like to meet the Indian,
M. Anantanarayanan.

I picture him as short and tan.
We'd meet, perhaps, in Hindustan.
I'd say, with admirable *élan*,
"Ah, Anantanarayanan—

I've heard of you. The *Times* once ran
A notice on your novel, an
Unusual tale of God and Man."
And Anantanarayanan

Would seat me on a lush divan
And read his name—that sumptuous span
Of "a's" and "n's" more lovely than
"In Xanadu did Kubla Khan"—

Aloud to me all day. I plan
Henceforth to be an ardent fan
Of Anantanarayanan—
M. Anantanarayanan.

AGATHA CHRISTIE
AND BEATRIX POTTER

Many-volumed authoresses
In capacious country dresses,
Full of cheerful art and nearly
Perfect craft, we love you dearly.

You know the hedgerow, stile, and barrow,
Have sniffed the cabbage, leek, and marrow,
Have heard the prim postmistress snicker,
And spied out murder in the vicar.

You've drawn the berry-beaded brambles
Where Mrs. Tiggy-Winkle rambles,
And mapped the attics in the village
Where mice plot alibis and pillage.

God bless you, girls, for in these places
You give us cozy scares and chases
That end with innocence acquitted—
Except for Cotton-tail, who did it.

MEDITATION ON A NEWS ITEM

Fidel Castro, who considers himself first in war
and first in peace, was first in the Hemingway
fishing tourney at Havana, Cuba. "I am a novice
at fishing," said Fidel. "You are a lucky novice,"
replied Ernest.
—*Life, in June, 1960*

Yes, yes, and there is even a photograph,
of the two in profile, both bearded, both sharp-nosed,
both (though the one is not wearing a cap
and the other is not carrying a cat)
magnificently recognizable (do
you think that much-photographed faces grow
larger, more deeply themselves, like flowers
in sunlight?). A great cup sits between their chests.

Life does not seem to think it very strange.
It runs the shot cropped to four inches,
and the explanation is given in full above.
But to me it seems immeasurably strange: as strange
to me as if there were found,
in a Jacobean archive, an unquestionably authentic
woodcut showing Shakespeare
presenting the blue ribbon for Best Cake Baked
to Queen Elizabeth.

And even the dialogue: so perfect—

"You are a lucky novice." Succinct,
wry, ominous, innocent: Nick Adams talking.
How did it happen? Did he,
convulsively departing from the exhausting regimen—
the rising at 6 a.m. to sharpen twelve pencils
with which to cut, as he stands at his bookcase,
269 or 312 or 451 more words into the paper
that will compose one of those many rumored books
that somehow never appear—did he abruptly exclaim,
"I must have a fishing tourney!"
and have posters painted and posted
in cabañas, cigar stores, and bordellos,
ERNEST HEMINGWAY FISHING COMPETITION,
just like that?

And did he receive, on one of those soft Havana mornings,
while the smoky-green Caribbean laps the wharf legs,
and the *señoritas* yawn behind grillwork,
and the black mailmen walk in khaki shorts,
an application blank stating CASTRO, Fidel?
Occupation: Dictator. *Address:*
Top Floor, Habana-Hilton Hotel (commandeered).
Hobbies: Ranting, U.S.-Baiting, Fishing (novice).

And was it honest? I mean, did Castro
wade down off the beach in hip boots
in a long cursing line of other contestants, Cubans,
cabdrivers, pimps, restaurant waiters, small landowners,
and make his cast, the bobbin singing,
and the great fish leap, with a splash
leap from the smoky-green waves,
and he, tugging, writhing, bring it in

38

and stand there, mopping the brow
of his somehow fragile, Apollonian profile
while the great man panted back and forth
plying his tape measure?

And at the award ceremony,
did their two so-different sorts of fame—
yet tangent on the point of beards and love of exploit—
create in the air one of those eccentric electronic
        disturbances
to which our younger physicists devote so much thought?
In the photograph, there is some sign of it:
they seem beatified, and resemble
two apostles by Dürer, possibly Peter and Paul.

My mind sinks down through the layers of strangeness:
I am as happy as if I had opened
a copy of "Alice in Wonderland"
in which the heroine *does* win the croquet contest
administered by the Queen of Hearts.

II

TELEPHONE POLES

They have been with us a long time.
They will outlast the elms.
Our eyes, like the eyes of a savage sieving the trees
In his search for game,
Run through them. They blend along small-town streets
Like a race of giants that have faded into mere mythology.
Our eyes, washed clean of belief,
Lift incredulous to their fearsome crowns of bolts, trusses,
      struts, nuts, insulators, and such
Barnacles as compose
These weathered encrustations of electrical debris—
Each a Gorgon's head, which, seized right,
Could stun us to stone.

Yet they are ours. We made them.
See here, where the cleats of linemen
Have roughened a second bark
Onto the bald trunk. And these spikes
Have been driven sideways at intervals handy for human
      legs.
The Nature of our construction is in every way
A better fit than the Nature it displaces.
What other tree can you climb where the birds' twitter,
Unscrambled, is English? True, their thin shade is negligible,
But then again there is not that tragic autumnal
Casting-off of leaves to outface annually.
These giants are more constant than evergreens
By being never green.

WASH

For seven days it rained that June;
A storm half out to sea kept turning around like a dog
      trying to settle himself on a rug;
We were the fleas that complained in his hair.

On the eighth day, before I had risen,
My neighbors' clothes had rushed into all the back yards
And lifted up their arms in praise.

From an upstairs window it seemed prehistorical:
Through the sheds and fences and vegetable gardens,
Workshirts and nightgowns, long-soaked in the cellar,

Underpants, striped towels, diapers, child's overalls,
Bibs and black bras thronging the sunshine
With hosannas of cotton and halleluiahs of wool.

THE SHORT DAYS

I like the way, in winter, cars
Ignite beneath the lingering stars
And, with a cough or two, unpark,
And roar to work still in the dark.

Like some great father, slugabed,
Whose children crack the dawn with play,
The sun retains a heavy head
Behind the hill, and stalls the day.

Then red rims gild the gutter-spouts;
The streetlamp pales; the milk-truck fades;
And housewives—husbands gone—wash doubts
Down sinks and raise the glowing shades.

The cars are gone, they will return
When headlights in a new night burn;
Between long drinks of Acheron
The thirst of broad day has begun.

SUBURBAN MADRIGAL

Sitting here in my house,
looking through my windows
diagonally at my neighbor's house,
I see his sun-porch windows;
they are filled with blue-green,
the blue-green of my car,
which I parked in front of my house,
more or less, up the street,
where I can't directly see it.

How promiscuous is
the world of appearances!
How frail are property laws!
To him his window is filled with his
things: his lamps, his plants, his radio.
How annoyed he would be to know
that my car, legally parked,
yet violates his windows,
paints them full
(to me) of myself, my car,
my well-insured '55 Fordor Ford
a gorgeous green sunset streaking his panes.

MOSQUITO

On the fine wire of her whine she walked,
Unseen in the ominous bedroom dark.
A traitor to her camouflage, she talked
A thirsty blue streak distinct as a spark.

I was to her a fragrant lake of blood
From which she had to sip a drop or die.
A reservoir, a lavish field of food,
I lay awake, unconscious of my size.

We seemed fair-matched opponents. Soft she dropped
Down like an anchor on her thread of song.
Her nose sank thankfully in; then I slapped
At the sting on my arm, cunning and strong.

A cunning, strong Gargantua, I struck
This lover pinned in the feast of my flesh,
Lulled by my blood, relaxed, half-sated, stuck
Engrossed in the gross rivers of myself.

Success! Without a cry the creature died,
Became a fleck of fluff upon the sheet.
The small welt of remorse subsides as side
By side we, murderer and murdered, sleep.

EARTHWORM

We pattern our Heaven
on bright butterflies,
but it must be that even
in earth Heaven lies.

The worm we uproot
in turning a spade
returns, careful brute,
to the peace he has made.

God blesses him; he
gives praise with his toil,
lends comfort to me,
and aërates the soil.

Immersed in the facts,
one must worship there;
claustrophobia attacks
us even in air.

CALENDAR

Toward August's end,
a hard night rain;
and the lawn is littered
with leaves again.

How the seasons blend!
So seeming still,
summer is fettered
to a solar will

which never rests.
The slanting ray
ignites migration
within the jay

and plans for nests
are hatching when
the northern nation
looks white to men.

SEAGULLS

A gull, up close,
looks surprisingly stuffed.
His fluffy chest seems filled
with an inexpensive taxidermist's material
rather lumpily inserted. The legs,
unbent, are childish crayon strokes—
too simple to be workable.
And even the feather-markings,
whose intricate symmetry is the usual glory of birds,
are in the gull slovenly,
as if God makes too many
to make them very well.

Are they intelligent?
We imagine so, because they are ugly.
The sardonic one-eyed profile, slightly cross,
the narrow, ectomorphic head, badly combed,
the wide and nervous and well-muscled rump
all suggest deskwork: shipping rates
by day, Schopenhauer
by night, and endless coffee.

At that hour on the beach
when the flies begin biting in the renewed coolness
and the backsliding skin of the after-surf
reflects a pink shimmer before being blotted,
the gulls stand around in the dimpled sand

like those melancholy European crowds
that gather in cobbled public squares in the wake
of assassinations and invasions,
heads cocked to hear the latest radio reports.

It is also this hour when plump young couples
walk down to the water, bumping together,
and stand thigh-deep in the rhythmic glass.
Then they walk back toward the car,
tugging as if at a secret between them,
but which neither quite knows;
walk capricious paths through the scattering gulls,
as in some mythologies
beautiful gods stroll unconcerned
among our mortal apprehensions.

MAPLES IN A SPRUCE FOREST

They live by attenuation,
Straining, vine-thin,
Up to gaps their gold leaves crowd
Like drowning faces surfacing.

Wherever dappled sun persists,
Shy leaves work photosynthesis;
Until I saw these slender doomed,
I did not know what a maple is.

The life that plumps the oval
In the open meadow full
Is beggared here, distended toward
The dying light available.

Maturity of sullen spruce
Will murder these deciduous;
A little while, the fretted gloom
Is dappled with chartreuse.

VERMONT

Here green is king again,
Usurping honest men.
Like Brazilian cathedrals gone under to creepers,
Gray silos mourn their keepers.

Here ski tows
And shy cows
Alone pin the ragged slopes to the earth
Of profitable worth.

Hawks, professors,
And summering ministers
Roost on the mountainsides of poverty
And sniff the poetry,

And every year
The big black bear,
Slavering through the woods with scrolling mouth,
Comes further south.

HOEING

I sometimes fear the younger generation will be deprived
   of the pleasures of hoeing;
   there is no knowing
how many souls have been formed by this simple exercise.

The dry earth like a great scab breaks, revealing
   moist-dark loam—
   the pea-root's home,
a fertile wound perpetually healing.

How neatly the green weeds go under!
   The blade chops the earth new.
   Ignorant the wise boy who
has never performed this simple, stupid, and useful wonder.

HOW TO BE UNCLE SAM

My father knew
   how to be
      Uncle Sam.

Six feet two,
   he led the
      parade

the year
   the boys came back
      from war.

Splendidly
   spatted, his legs
      like canes,

his dandy coat
   like a
      bluebird's back,

he led the parade,
   and then
      a man

(I've never been sure
   he was honestly
      canned—

he might have been
    consciously
        after a laugh)

popped
    from the crowd,
        swinging his hands,

and screamed,
    "You're the s.o.b.
        who takes

all my money!"
    and took
        a poke at

my own father.
    He missed
        by half

an inch; he felt
    the wind, my father
        later said.

When the cops
    grabbed that one,
        another man

shouted from the
    crowd in a
        voice like brass:

"I don't care if
    you take a poke at
        Updike,

but don't you
bother
Uncle Sam!"

FEBRUARY 22

Three boys, American, in dungarees,
walk at a slant across the street
against the mild slant of the winter sun,
moseying out this small, still holiday.

The back of the cold is broken; later snows
will follow, mixed with rain, but today
the macadam is bare, the sun loops high,
and the trees are bathed in sweet grayness.

He was a perfect hero: a man of stone,
as colorless as a monument,
anonymous as Shakespeare. We know him
only as the author of his deeds.

There may have been a man: a surveyor,
a wencher, a temper, a stubborn farmer's mind;
but our legends seem impertinent
gaieties scratched upon his granite.

He gazes at us from our dollar bills
reproachfully, a strange green lady,
heavy-lidded, niggle-lipped, and wigged,
who served us better than we have deserved.

More than great successes, we love great failures.
Lincoln is Messiah; he, merely Caesar.
He suffered greatness like a curse.
He fathered our country, we feel, without great joy.

But let us love him now, for he crossed the famous ice,
brought us out of winter, stood, and surveyed
the breadth of our land exulting in the sun:
looked forward to the summer that is past. .

SHILLINGTON

The vacant lots are occupied, the woods
Diminish, Slate Hill sinks beneath its crown
Of solvent homes, and marketable goods
On all sides crowd the good remembered town.

Returning, we find our snapshots inexact.
Perhaps a condition of being alive
Is that the clothes which, setting out, we packed
With love no longer fit when we arrive.

Yet sights that limited our truth were strange
To older eyes; the town that we have lost
Is being found by hands that still arrange
Horse chestnut heaps and fingerpaint on frost.

Time shades these alleys; every pavement crack
Is mapped somewhere. A solemn concrete ball,
On the gatepost of a sold house, brings back
A waist leaning against a buckling wall.

The gutter-fires smoke, their burning done
Except for, fanned within, an orange feather;
We have one home, the first, and leave that one.
The having and leaving go on together.

Written for the semicentennial celebration of this borough's
incorporation in 1908.

MOVIE HOUSE

View it, by day, from the back,
from the parking lot in the rear,
for from this angle only
the beautiful brick blankness can be grasped.
Monumentality
wears one face in all ages.

No windows intrude real light
into this temple of shades,
and the size of it,
the size of the great rear wall measures
the breadth of the dreams we have had here.
It dwarfs the village bank,
outlooms the town hall,
and even in its decline
makes the bright-ceilinged supermarket seem mean.

Stark closet of stealthy rapture,
vast introspective camera
wherein our most daring self-projections
were given familiar names:
stand, stand by your macadam lake
and tell the aeons of our extinction
that we too could house our gods,
could secrete a pyramid
to sight the stars by.

OLD-FASHIONED
LIGHTNING ROD

Green upright rope
of copper, sprouting
(from my perspective) from
an amber ball—jaundiced amber,
the belly-bulb
of an old grasshopper—
braced between three
sturdy curlicues of wrought
iron (like elegancies
of logical thought)
and culminating—the rod,
the slender wand of spiral
copper weathered pistachio-pale—
in a crown, a star
of five radiating thorns
honed fine on the fine-grained
grinding blue wheel of sky:
flared fingers, a torch,
a gesture, crying,
"I dare you!"

THE STUNT FLIER

I come into my dim bedroom
innocently and my baby
is lying in her crib face-down;
just a hemisphere of the half-bald head
shows, and the bare feet, uncovered,
the small feet crossed at the ankles
like a dancer doing easily
a difficult step—or,
more exactly, like a cherub
planing through Heaven,
cruising at a middle altitude
through the cumulus of the tumbled covers,
which disclose the feet crossed
at the ankles *à la* small boys who,
exulting in their mastery of bicycles,
lift their hands from the handle bars
to demonstrate how easy gliding is.

THE FRITILLARY

The fritillary,
Fickle, wary,
Flits from plant to plant with nary
A forethought as to where he
Alights, a butterfly.

And, what's extraordinary,
Is also an herb—
The same word serves.
Nothing disturbs
Its thick green nerves.

When one lights on the other it is very
Nice:
The spotted wings and the spotted petals, both
  spelled from the Latin *fritillus* [dice],
Nod together
Toward a center
Where a mirror
Might be imagined.
They are tangent,
Self to self, the same
Within a single name.
The miracle has occurred.

Alas! The wingèd word
With a blind flap leaves the leaved,
Unbereaved,
And bobbles down the breeze,
Careless of etymologies.

MOBILE OF BIRDS

There is something
in their planetary weave that is comforting.

The polycentric orbits, elliptical
with mutual motion,
random as nature, and yet, above all,
calculable, recall
those old Ptolemaic heavens small
enough for the Byzantine Trinity,
    Plato's Ideals,
     formal devotion,
seven levels of bliss, and numberless wheels
of omen, balanced occultly.

                        A small bird
at an arc's extremity
adequately weights
his larger mates'
compounded mass: absurd
but actual—there he floats!

Persisting through a doorway, shadow-casting light
    dissolves on the wall
    the mobile's threads
and turns its spatial conversation
dialectical. Silhouettes,
projections of identities,

merge and part and reunite
in shapely syntheses—
                              an illusion,
for the birds on their perches of fine wire avoid collusion
and are twirled
alone in their suspenseful world.

LES SAINTS NOUVEAUX

Proust, doing penance
in a cork-lined room,
numbered the petals
in the orchards of doom
and sighed through the vortex
of his own strained breath
the wonderfully abundant
perfume called Death.

Brancusi, an anchorite
among rough shapes,
blessed each with his eyes
until like grapes
they popped, releasing
kernels of motion
as patiently worked
as if by the ocean.

Cézanne, grave man,
pondered the scene
and saw it with passion
as orange and green,
and weighted his strokes
with days of decision,
and founded on apples
theologies of vision.

DIE NEUEN HEILIGEN

Kierkegaard, a
cripple and a Dane,
disdained to marry;
the consequent strain
unsprung the whirling
gay knives of his wits,
which slashed the Ideal
and himself to bits.

Kafka, a lawyer
and citizen of Prague,
became consumptive
in the metaphysic fog
and, coughing with laughter,
lampooned the sad state
that judged its defendants
all guilty of Fate.

Karl Barth, more healthy,
and married, and Swiss,
lived longer, yet took
small comfort from this;
Nein! he cried, rooting
in utter despair
the Credo that Culture
left up in the air.

TREES EAT SUNSHINE

It's the fact:
their broad leaves lap it up like milk
and turn it into twigs.

Fish eat fish.
Lamps eat light
and when their feast has starved their filament
go out.

So do we,
and all sweet creatures—
cats eating horses, horses grass, grass earth, earth
       water—
except for the distant Man

who inhales the savor of souls—
let us all strive to resemble this giant!

FEVER

I have brought back a good message from the land of 102°:
God exists.
I had seriously doubted it before;
but the bedposts spoke of it with utmost confidence,
the threads in my blanket took it for granted,
the tree outside the window dismissed all complaints,
and I have not slept so justly for years.
It is hard, now, to convey
how emblematically appearances sat
upon the membranes of my consciousness;
but it is a truth long known,
that some secrets are hidden from health.

SEVEN STANZAS AT EASTER

Make no mistake: if He rose at all
it was as His body;
if the cells' dissolution did not reverse, the molecules
    reknit, the amino acids rekindle,
the Church will fall.

It was not as the flowers,
each soft Spring recurrent;
it was not as His Spirit in the mouths and fuddled
    eyes of the eleven apostles;
it was as His flesh: ours.

The same hinged thumbs and toes,
the same valved heart
that—pierced—died, withered, paused, and then
    regathered out of enduring Might
new strength to enclose.

Let us not mock God with metaphor,
analogy, sidestepping, transcendence;
making of the event a parable, a sign painted in the
    faded credulity of earlier ages:
let us walk through the door.

The stone is rolled back, not papier-mâché,
not a stone in a story,

but the vast rock of materiality that in the slow
    grinding of time will eclipse for each of us
the wide light of day.

And if we will have an angel at the tomb,
make it a real angel,
weighty with Max Planck's quanta, vivid with hair,
    opaque in the dawn light, robed in real linen
spun on a definite loom.

Let us not seek to make it less monstrous,
for our own convenience, our own sense of beauty,
lest, awakened in one unthinkable hour, we are
    embarrassed by the miracle,
and crushed by remonstrance.

Written for a religious arts festival sponsored by the Clifton
Lutheran Church, of Marblehead, Mass.

VIBRATION

The world vibrates, my sleepless nights
discovered. The air conditioner hummed;
I turned it off. The plumbing
in the next apartment sang;
I moved away, and found a town
whose factories shuddered as they worked
all night. The wires on the poles
outside my windows quivered in an ecstasy
stretched thin between horizons.
I went to where no wires were; and there,
as I lay still, a dragon tremor
seized my darkened body, gnawed
my heart, and murmured, *I am you.*

MODIGLIANI'S DEATH MASK

Fogg Museum, Cambridge

The shell of a doll's head,
It stares askew, lopsided in death,
With nervous lips, a dirty tan,
And no bigger than my hand.
Could the man have been that small?
Or is life, like rapid motion,
An enlarging illusion?
Ringed, Italianly, with ivy,
The mask makes an effect of litter,
Preserved inside its glass case like
An oddly favored grapefruit rind.

SUMMER: WEST SIDE

When on the coral-red steps of old brownstones
Puerto Rican boys, their white shirts luminous,
gather, and their laughter
conveys menace as far as Central Park West,

When the cheesecake shops on Broadway
keep open long into the dark,
and the Chinaman down in his hole of seven steps
leaves the door of his laundry ajar,
releasing a blue smell of starch,

When the indefatigable lines of parked cars
seem embedded in the tar,
and the swish of the cars on the Drive
seems urgently loud—

Then even the lapping of wavelets
on the boards of a barge on the Hudson
is audible,
and Downtown's foggy glow
fills your windows right up to the top.

And you walk in the mornings with your cool suit
sheathing the fresh tingle of your shower,
and the gratings idly steam,
and the damp path of the street-sweeper evaporates,

And—an oddly joyful sight—
the dentists' and chiropractors' white signs low
in the windows of the great ochre buildings on Eighty-
   sixth Street
seem slightly darkened
by one more night's deposit of vigil.

3 A.M.

By the brilliant ramp
of a ceaseless garage

the eye like a piece of newspaper
staring from a collage

records on a yellowing
gridwork of nerve

"policemen move on feet of glue,
sailors stick to the curb."

EROTIC EPIGRAMS

I

The landscape of love
can only be seen
through a slim windowpane
one's own breath fogs.

II

Iseult, to Tristan
(condemned to die),
is like a letter of reprieve
which is never delivered
but he knows has been dispatched.

III

Hoping to fashion a mirror, the lover
doth polish the face of his beloved
until he produces a skull.

FLIRT

The flirt is an antelope of flame,
igniting the plain
wherever she hesitates.
She kisses my wrist, waits,
and watches the flush of pride
absurdly kindle my eyes.
She talks in riddles,
exposes her middle,
is hard and strange in my arms:
I love her. Her charms
are those of a fine old book with half-cut pages,
bound in warm plush at her white neck's nape.

THE BLESSING

The room darkened, darkened until
our nakedness was a form of gray;
then the rain came bursting,
and we were sheltered, blessed,
upheld in a world of elements
that held us justified.
In all the love I had felt for you before,
in all that love,
there was no love
like that I felt when the rain began:
dim room, enveloping rush,
the slenderness of your throat,
the blessèd slenderness.

THE GREAT SCARF OF BIRDS

Playing golf on Cape Ann in October,
I saw something to remember.

Ripe apples were caught like red fish in the nets
of their branches. The maples
were colored like apples,
part orange and red, part green.
The elms, already transparent trees,
seemed swaying vases full of sky. The sky
was dramatic with great straggling V's
of geese streaming south, mare's-tails above them.
Their trumpeting made us look up and around.
The course sloped into salt marshes,
and this seemed to cause the abundance of birds.

As if out of the Bible
or science fiction,
a cloud appeared, a cloud of dots
like iron filings which a magnet
underneath the paper undulates.
It dartingly darkened in spots,
paled, pulsed, compressed, distended, yet
held an identity firm: a flock
of starlings, as much one thing as a rock.
One will moved above the trees
the liquid and hesitant drift.

Come nearer, it became less marvellous,

more legible, and merely huge.
"I never saw so many birds!" my friend exclaimed.
We returned our eyes to the game.
Later, as Lot's wife must have done,
in a pause of walking, not thinking
of calling down a consequence,
I lazily looked around.

The rise of the fairway above us was tinted,
so evenly tinted I might not have noticed
but that at the rim of the delicate shadow
the starlings were thicker and outlined the flock
as an inkstain in drying pronounces its edges.
The gradual rise of green was vastly covered;
I had thought nothing in nature could be so broad
  but grass.

And as
I watched, one bird,
prompted by accident or will to lead,
ceased resting; and, lifting in a casual billow,
the flock ascended as a lady's scarf,
transparent, of gray, might be twitched
by one corner, drawn upward and then,
decided against, negligently tossed toward a chair:
the southward cloud withdrew into the air.

Long had it been since my heart
had been lifted as it was by the lifting of that great
  scarf.

WINTER OCEAN

Many-maned scud-thumper, tub
of male whales, maker of worn wood, shrub-
ruster, sky-mocker, rave!
portly pusher of waves, wind-slave.

A Note on the Type

THE TEXT of this book was set on the Linotype in JANSON, a recutting made direct from type cast from matrices long thought to have been made by the Dutchman Anton Janson, who was a practicing type founder in Leipzig during the years 1668–87. However, it has been conclusively demonstrated that these types are actually the work of Nicholas Kis (1650–1702), a Hungarian, who most probably learned his trade from the master Dutch type founder Dirk Voskens. The type is an excellent example of the influential and sturdy Dutch types that prevailed in England up to the time William Caslon developed his own incomparable designs from these Dutch faces.

A Note about the Author

JOHN UPDIKE was born in 1932, in Shillington, Pennsylvania. He graduated from Harvard College in 1954, and from 1955 to 1957 was a member of the staff of *The New Yorker*, to which he has contributed short stories, poems, and humor. Presently he lives, with his wife and their four children, in Ipswich, Massachusetts.

September 1963